My Life In Real Times

Short Stories with Long Lessons

WILLIAM F. NOLAN SR.

Published by Toni Hatton Productions
www.tonihatton.com

My Life in Real Times
Short Stories with Long Lessons
©2013 by William F. Nolan Sr.

All rights reserved. No part of this publication may be reproduced or transmitted in any form or by any means, electronic or mechanical, including photocopying, recording, or by any information storage and retrieval system, without the prior written permission from the publisher or the author. Contact the publisher for information on foreign rights.

ISBN: 978-1-4507-8310-1

Printed in the United States of America

Dedication

Children are special gifts to us all. They make us laugh and they make us cry. Sometimes you wonder what to do with them. They are what we asked for and they become the joy of our lives. My children are far and near. Love never dies. They need us daily if only in phone conversation. No matter how old they get, they are the gifts that we asked for. I'm thankful to welcome them into my life. I dedicate this book to my 5 special gifts from the Almighty, William Jr., Toni, Michelle, Charles, and Jason!

Introduction

Most of my life, I've told stories to people and they found them to be very funny! When my children came along, I told them ghostly stories to put them to sleep after a long ride home. Later, I would write about things that I noticed on the streets. I found these stories rewarding and true. That's what I like, true stories, stories that make people reflect on life's rewards and promises from the God of all people. He guides my hand and controls my thoughts. I present words that I hope will give people a new look at what they're seeing in a world filled with crossroads and many challenges. Pick a road from my book and hopefully it will take you to new levels in a world that's willing to give to you all that you ask for. I encourage you to read a story a day, reflect, meditate, and journal about it. I've included some thought-provoking questions in the back of this book that will assist you in searching the deep reservoirs of your heart and mind and discover, activate, and manifest your true authentic power to create a life that rewards you and adds value to the lives of others!

Table of Contents

Affirmations 1

Personalities 2

Broken Bridges 3

Commitment 4

Winds of the Mind 5

Maximize Your Time 6

Searching for Purpose 7

Hang Your Hat 8

Break the Chains 9

Passion to Succeed 10

Choices 11

Boredom 12

Power of Intention 13

Start Anew   15

Loaned Material   16

Fear   17

New Steps   18

A Good Life   19

The Soul of Man   20

The Flow   21

The Challenge   22

Life's road   23

Moving on   24

No Regrets   25

A Better Life   26

Differences   27

Change   28

Memories   29

Abundant Life   30

Vision   31

Deal With It!   33

Idle Minds   34

What a Waste!   35

The Brain   36

Our Words   37

Defining Choices   38

Thoughts   39

Life's Formula   40

Dreaming Again?   41

Role Models   42

Motivated   43

Relationships   45

Memories   46

The Storms of Life   47

Respect   48

So Much More   49

The Wind   50

Reflections   51

Heroes   52

Roadmap to Success   53

A Still Pond   54

Have a Seat!   55

Hard Times   56

Where We Are   57

Life   58

Quiet Places   59

Real Purpose   60

Be Remembered   61

Investment   62

Limitless   63

Free to Choose   64

The Left Behinds   65

I'll Fly Away!   66

Acknowledgements   67

Master Your Mind!   69

Affirmations

Affirmations create positive lifestyles! Having a good day requires something as simple as just getting started. We create our own balance and our own lives. If we cry, we feel one way. If we laugh, we feel another way. See my point! If we stay in a frame of mind that creates positive thinking, we will always be ready for that time when life's challenges show up in our lives. You create positive thinking by practicing it over and over again. Tell yourself, "I'm better than this! I will not bend to this situation because it's not good for me!" Say this to yourself, listen to what you say, weigh the benefits, and oppose the downside. Now, you be the judge. We all need help because every day is a learning experience and we must deal with it if we are going to stay in the race. So start today! Try some of these affirmations. This is the day to try out your new mantra and stick with it. "Today is going to be the best day of my life!" If we keep saying positive affirmations and believe what we say, all of these affirmations will be cemented in our lives forever!

Personalities

Personalities are real! Do you love them or do you just accept them? What do you think? Can you stand yourself? What's your personality? Are you easy to get along with or do you make people wonder and say, "What a pity!" We all have different lifestyles that could make us scream, but what the heck! Just deal with it because it's all we have. Nevertheless, there is something we can do to learn to enjoy people who have different points of view. We can learn so much more when we listen, participate, and interact. Everyone has something to say of interest that can be applied to life's situations. Sit down and say a few words to a stranger, either at work or in a social setting and watch the conversation flow! Everyone desires to be heard and tell their story. I hear them all the time. So, the next time you are out and about, say to someone, "Nice day today!" Then, watch the response you get! Well, good luck! Keep making friends. Who knows, we may meet some day!

Broken Bridges

How many bridges have you crossed in your life? Did you burn them all or are they still somewhere in the distance? We walk through life leaving a paper trail. Sometimes it's seen by a stranger and sometimes by a loved one. Are we at our best when we are seen or are we breezing just to get by? Will we ever get to the mountain top of life to really see the world as it sees us? Inside of our mind is a world of knowledge. I'm tapping into mine as I write. Free yourself of all the things that keep you from looking back in the distance and seeing those bridges. Burn the ones that have failed and close the gap to the ones that need fixing. Soon you'll see in the distance someone working from the other side. Bridges to the mind and bridges to the heart… Same difference… Get started!

Commitment

Have you ever started a project and never finished? Why did you stop? Did you feel strong enough to stay tuned? Well, long-term commitment is the answer when we start a new project. It's important to stay the course. When we shift from place to place we're telling ourselves it's okay to change when things get tough. But, it's not so! The only way to reach your goal in life is to be strong in your values to yourself. Others will not care if you fail or succeed. It's not there concern. Therefore, it's you and only you that will stand the test of time. Take a moment to capture the essence of your mind and move forward with your choices in life. The bottom line will put you where you desire to be!

…over the top

Winds of the Mind

Grab the wind and take a ride into your destiny! Call on the subtle parts of the mind and discover the true you. These are the areas that can't be seen or understood unless we quiet the mind and let the flow begin. The deeper you go better it becomes. So, take the trip and learn all that you've been missing. See colors brighter! Smell the aromas deeper! This is your home. Learn to live in it. Give it a permanent address and call this place of mystic value my dwelling place!

Maximize Your Time

Wasting time is a terrible thing to do! There are so many other ways to move time and to do something positive. We shouldn't give up precious moments to a situation that gives nothing in return such as toxic relationships that go nowhere and poor conversation that lacks any new information. ...same road, same track, and the same bull! Move on to a better place, more pleasant times, and new faces! I will promise you that the sun shines brighter when the obstacles are removed. Food taste better when you eat! Sleep feels better when you awake! It's time to set sail. There's a nice breeze that is coming your way and a large ocean waiting to take you to a place of new beginnings and calmer waters!

Searching for Purpose

Do you ever sit down and try to figure out life, your purpose, and where it's all going? Well, I do and I still can't find the answers. I mean, you listen to people and there's still not enough to know. I must say that I believe there is a formula to follow to be successful and it's no secret! We all have the ability to make it happen. But we must stay the course and never waiver. The road will be long, I must say. Now back to the mystery of God… Where is God? We see what He has created but where is God? They say He is Spirit and can't be seen with human eyes. He judges each of us. I pray that one day my God will enlighten me so that I can be a strong follower. I will keep searching for the answers and I will find the way!

Hang Your Hat

Hats are for hat racks. Have you ever heard this before, "Use your head for something other than a hat rack"! Man, that's powerful talk and a message we all can listen to! Let's see, a hat rack for a head... That includes a brain, eyes, ears, a nose, and most of the things we need to survive. Is it just a hat rack? Come on! Well, the truth is most people do. We walk around and leave life's gifts to other people. When we learn something we enrich our lives and are able to pass it on along with the skills that are needed to deal with every day realities. Put the "hat rack" thought out of your mind and fill your brain with the gift of learning. Go through life knowing that you are prepared to deal with whatever comes your way because the gift, once learned, will never leave you. Leave the hat on the rack by the door and use the head on your shoulders!

Break the Chains

Ever had a friend that stays angry? Well, I know of such a person. I believe that they see the world most of the time, different from everyday people. Their vision is distorted and everyone is the enemy. I've worked hard at trying to break through for eight years and I'm still trying. What makes people see the world that way? There are a lot of good people. We have to work at finding them. They're not in old neighborhoods where only the depressed are left behind. They will not be found at work where there's very little contact because some are worse than the ones in the old neighborhoods. I think we all will benefit when we internalize and find the real person that we were meant to be from the beginning of time, created by the God of all gods. When we fail to see the freedom of a new life, we instead stay smothered in a sauce that's not fit for human consumption. We must break the chains of anger and reroute it to a direction that will uplift us to a level of no return. All of these gifts are here inside of us and they are ours for the taking. We must work to learn the rules of life lessons, the ones that will give us a new day!

Passion to Succeed

Passion to succeed… treat it like your life depends on it! When we want something bad enough, a new chemistry develops and flows like a mighty river inside of us. This chemistry lies dormant sometimes for years, until one day the need for it appears. When we get that feeling, look out! Everything takes a backseat and off we go. Whether it concerns a relationship, a new job, a house, or anything that's strong enough to drive us to seek and find our rewards, we all have this drive. Many choose not to seek the jewel designed to set us free from life's horrors. These passionate chemical fluids flow in slow motion at all times, waiting to be released into the real world where it was designed to be. Self contained humans loaded with prosperity, is what we are. All we have to do is unlock the doors that contain this internal monster. So, think about what your passion might be and release this lifelong companion. You'll see the rewards come charging right at you, now, tomorrow, and whenever you decide to release the fluids of your passion!

Choices

One young lady carrying books while another carries a baby. Both are young and bright and about 19 years old. What I'm talking about here is the choices that shape our lives. We all want what's best for us in this life, (So true!) but sometimes we cross paths with the wrong people and a course that we never dreamed possible takes us down the trail depression and despair all because of our choices. Our family and upbringing has a lot to do with our outcome in life. Good fathers, good mothers, and education all work hand-in-hand and determine how we develop. Sometimes young man deliver a dead blow to the young women and because of this, she falls the wrong way. So our choices have to be more directly favorable to our well-being. Make good choices in life and the outcome will be appreciated!

Boredom

When we become bored, the brain gets excited for activity and has a need to do something stimulating. This is the human nature that kicks in. So, what do we do? For some, they respond by doing something to stay busy like watch the television, read, or take a long walk. Others still will not find this as a good source. So they just do nothing, and let their thoughts run wild. Dealing with the mind is a job 24/7. Even when we're so called asleep, there is still activity going on. There are dreams that we live out as we sleep. So, we are ever present in thought, even though we are not aware during the sleep mode. Stimulation is good for all parts of the body. The joints require a certain amount of flexibility to stay in tune. It's our body and we are the keepers of our own castle and must maintain it. Sometimes a long walk around the track at the local school will bring pleasure. Dancing, talking to friends on the phone, rearranging furniture, listening to music, or lifting weights will all minimize boredom and bring relief to a stilled mind. So, when you experience boredom, act right away! Move on it and watch activity do its homework!

Power of Intention

While watching TV late one night, Dr. Dyer talked about the power of intention. What caught my attention was the fact that what this man talked about I was already connected to. I'm referring to the plan for spiritual growth in life. I say plan because everything in life is preset to be what it was intended to be. I speak of the inner soul of man. This inner man is a direct connection to the Creator. The soul is aware of all that we do and it's like a dual being living in the external body along with man. When we do things that are not pleasing to God, the inner soul fights against all undo actions. Why? Is it that we are so in love with the external world? Everything we see we see as exciting and don't see the need to do anything else. Wrong! Remember the soul man? What about the role it plays in your destiny? As we go through life, this dual relationship is external and there is no separation. No matter what we do in life there will always be internal opposition, the struggle between the internal and external man until these two

Godly creatures become one. A lost soul will always go through life, trying to disconnect with the soul of itself. It's only when they become one that God reveals Himself!

Start Anew

Can we do this at this point in our lives? Yes! Changing the course of life is like a ship on rough seas. In order to smooth the ride, change is a must. If life's rocky roads are flipping you around, then we must go deeper and internalize our thoughts. Go to a level of thought that is beyond the surface. This is where authentic thoughts are produced. We often never look to this area for help because as humans, we only use 10% of our potential in life until something happens and forces us to search for answers. It always starts way down in deep thought where the oceans of the mind rest in readiness to help you challenge life's rough courses. So, take a minute, sit in a quiet place, and let your thoughts tell you what's not going well in your life. Then all of a sudden, bingo, all things possible will become a reality. When you return from your thoughts, there will always be room for a new you!

Loaned Material

Minutes… Seconds… Hours… That's all we have in this life to hold onto! The clock ticks and we run to and fro, chasing time. Have you ever stopped and thought about life and the reason why we are here? I have and I'm still trying to get to where I need to be. We see signs all around us. Our friends are leaving this life and we never know who is going to be next. We rent our belongings for we will never take anything with us wherever we go. All of our earthly belongings are left to someone else. So, we don't own anything but our eternal spirit which is really one loan from God who has all of the possessions that we will need from this point on. So, will we say, "That's my house! That's my boat! That's my car! That's my wife! That's my dog!"? All of these gifts are really not ours. They are on loan from the God of creation!

Fear

When fear comes to your mind, do you panic, do you lose control, or do you just try to maintain self-discipline. We must do something or something will do us. I find that when fear looks at me, I say to myself, "What am I going to do?" At that point, I allow myself to really take control and deal with it because we can't live in fear or it will destroy us. We have to remember that unless it is on top of us we still have a chance to think our way out. So, don't panic if you're driving a car and you start to skid out of control. Don't worry about hitting a wall. Think about how to come out of the skid. In other words, you haven't hit the wall yet, so why think about it! Leave fear in a place where it has no power, out of your mind!

New Steps

Let me share something with you. When we live in an environment that speaks nothing but negative energy, we soon catch on to this way of life and may never let go of what's holding us to the old way of thinking. Stepping out of the box of life that chokes our growth will give us the freedom to learn new and rewarding steps towards better ways of fulfilling life's special calling for us as individuals.

A Good Life

Sometimes I question myself about what makes some people try to build a good life and others try to destroy a good life. It seems that when life becomes unbearable another side of the mind takes charge and a demon is released to do harm to all that are in the way. We don't do well when we are depressed. Our emotions take charge and our intellect takes a backseat. I believe that society is structured in such a way that it blocks progress for some and allows it for others. We are denied and become angry, striking out at everything around us. This is a lack of vision that we all have which can destroy the very fiber of man and leave him heartless. We all have to go to a place in our minds to find comfort and rest. For it is through this period of time that we must return to our conscious self and take on the challenges of our lives. Pain only lasts as long as you choose to endure it. We must move on and build new character. For this is the only chance that you have in this life!

The Soul of Man

When you're angry, your mind and your vision become distorted and there's no connection with your reality. If we're not careful we will fall into a frame of mind that may not return to its normal state. We want to maintain a positive mindset at all times. Sometimes a crisis takes place and the thought process skips a beat, which shifts us from being centered. We can only return when we begin to see a picture that is different from what we are experiencing at the moment. All powers come from within this mass that houses itself in the skulls of humans, which produces all that we need to know. We must learn to search our brain for our rewards are lying within, waiting to be discovered. No matter where we go or what we say, we will always be in direct contact with the gift from God, the Creator of all things big and small. I say keep thinking and learning how to deal with this life for as you learn, you grow and as you grow, you will connect to the soul of man!

The Flow

Life flows for some people and others tend to wander through life and never find that connection. I have found my connection and my peace follows me everywhere I go because we are one! In life, the foreseeable is what we want, but sometimes the unforeseeable is what we get! Hopefully it's all for the good!

The Challenge

Mastering your mind is a challenge! We only use 10% percentage of our brains true potential to guide us through this life, knowing there's so much more. Hidden in the darkness, the real essence of self is waiting to be discovered. Are you waiting to show the world that you too have the right stuff? Why do we ignore our possibilities of a better life and a better self, using only 10% of our true potential? Why?

Life's road

The road through life is long and hard all because of how we travel. Choosing off roads covered with thorn trails and deep forests will cause confusion and uncertainty. We continue the journey no matter what until the light shines no more. These are the days when we are unsure of where we want to be in this life. For some, this area of gray will last forever. Others will feel the pain earlier and move on to a more productive lifestyle. It's all about choices and the will to be better today than yesterday. Yes, life's roads tell the story of each of us. These roads are important to our rites of passage. When pain comes, it can be your friend. For when it hurts bad enough, it will cause us to move on. Hopefully it's to a place that's pain free!

Moving on

Moving on to a better you is the order of the day. For when we choose another course, we give ourselves a better chance of being who we really are. Some already know and others will discover what really makes them tick. Still, a new day will dawn and every day we live will challenge the next, over and over again. We are the keepers of the castle. We open the doors and close them at will. What makes this so difficult is the fact that we don't like change. Opportunities for change will come every day, some good and some we wish never existed. We always work towards what's better for us or at least we think so anyway. Again, choices are ours to ponder. When we look on to the better person, then and only then will we see daylight, smell the coffee, taste the sweet wines of a better tomorrow, a better you, and yes, the knowledge to try not to make the same wrong choices twice!

No Regrets

Happy are they that move on with no regrets! The ride was bitter and sweet and a better person emerged from the fire and sometimes joy. I think we come together because the inner persona wants love and peace and we go out searching for that sweet smell of a real person, someone who will share our feelings, our love, and yes, our new levels of height and success. Sometimes these awards come and we lose ourselves in the moments, hours, and eventually the years of joy and laughter. These times are great for most of us. Life smoothes out, the mind finds peace, and we move on until the storms come down. Then, people begin to come from everywhere, calling for you and calling for your mate. These are strange people moving about the edges of your life. Do you know why? They are the storms that we allow into our lives. When the joy wheel stops turning and the mind wanders, the storms that we all dread are showering down. Yes, happy are they that move on without regret. You will find that the raindrops, sunshine, and the sounds of lovebirds mating can still be heard! Blue skies will always appear! Yes, these are the rewards of moving on!

A Better Life

Why are you here? What are you seeking? Are you seeking something that defines you as a person? Is what you see causing you to move on to a better life? If so, then I have been of some help to you and to myself. Because of your growth, I have increased my awareness. Two wins in the same moment... But wait, there's more! Even after I'm gone, your knowledge will still bear fruit. We will always produce new levels, and there will be many. We must choose the ones that excite the inner person and that alone will bring rewards. Rise and shine for tomorrow is coming. As we make it through the night, we will see the forests, smell the fresh air, and hear the birds sing. With all of these joys, how could we go wrong in our quest to be the best we can be!

Differences

We're all different! We think differently. Our lifestyles are also different, but what makes us closely related is the way that God chose for us to be. No matter where we are we are still people of a greater God. He has planted in us the ability to communicate and to know right from wrong. Millions walk the earth with various looks, colors, heights, and gifts that are all designed for us to grow and prosper. Yes, these are material differences, but where God is concerned, we are all children of a greater God and he speaks at will no matter what!

Change

Can you change the person that you are? Do you see yourself as a person that needs to change? If so, would you choose to be better or would you choose to settle for less than the person that you are now? Change is a process that gives the brain chemistry a place of flow. Most people want to see a better day and a better person, a person who can make better decisions for themselves. Yes, change is a powerful word that plays a major role in the lives of people who see change as a way of fulfillment in a life that's getting shorter every day. If we can change just to have a little more and be a little more for ourselves, then change is the answer!

Memories

A new day has come and life resumes itself. We go to work, meet with friends, and have moments to ourselves. Just yesterday my friend left this world, never to return. I sit here reflecting on how we move about life, laughing, being carefree, and moving on with our lives. Life is full of memories from the past. Many of my friends are gone and I feel blessed to be here writing, working, caring for my family, and yes, giving thanks for the blessings that I've received. Life as we know it is a wonderful experience! We learn to do better for ourselves and hopefully, we meet people that can enjoy our presence. There's more to life than what we know. Most is hidden in the recesses of the brain, waiting to reveal itself to us at any time. But, we suppress our thoughts because of our daily routine, running here and there. Blessed are the ones that see beyond the moment for the end of the rainbow is still in view with treasures from around the world, shiny, sparkly, and real! They are waiting for you to grasp the extended life that most people miss in the moment! Yes, memories produce new realities. Sit for a while and visit the memories of your life. You might see the other side of that rainbow!

Abundant Life

What a beautiful world we live in! We grumble and complain to the point that we miss the real purpose of even being here. Celebrating life every day is a blessing that we experience all because we are alive and are able to fully function for ourselves. Still we cry for more! We are the makers of all we do. If we don't do it, we don't get it. Life in abundance is yours to hold onto, to develop your skills, and enjoy the bounty of God's creation. We will never stop complaining if we don't understand the realities of life that we are all exposed to. A new day will come and new dreams will come and go. Will we capture them and use them to be all that we can be in the land that allows freedom of choice to move about? Plan and receive the riches of the mind and the body that are already here in abundance for all of us to take and move forward!

Vision

When we have vision, we develop purpose of self! With vision, we see ourselves in the middle of our thoughts no matter if it's in school, in relationships, while building houses, or building ourselves. The main ingredient in vision is aspiring to be the God child that you were blessed to be. Everyone's purpose is to take them to higher levels of being. Somewhere along the way we get distracted because we lose our focus. We stop being in charge of our destiny and off we go towards the defeating actions of doing nothing about ourselves. Distractions can come from being in dysfunctional homes, and around friends who walk along the wild side of life. All of these experiences lead to defeat. Somewhere along the way we must get back on track because our vision has to become our focus. One will never see the best of one's self if there's no trying or staying true to one's course. As we begin to test our worth, gifts will begin to reveal themselves! We all need help with focusing on our vision because the world is full of distractions. Reading a self-help book and being around people of like minds can bring the best out of you. Again, we must try to reach the goals we aspire to reach and live that vision day in and day out! Remember, God started your life and he will guide you if you ask for his blessing!

Deal With It!

Everyone views life differently! Some see the real rewards that give us prosperity. Others see life through tunnel vision and their rewards are very dismal. What makes this happen is the way that we perceive life as individuals. There's a universal connection between people and as we tap into the mind it causes things to come together. Although we are all one, we might see things differently, but the power to understand life's mysteries are for all if only we connect!

Idle Minds

Idle minds produce negative thoughts! When we're not focusing, we're like dust in the wind, blowing to and fro. We end up gathering nothing as we move through life's highs and lows. We fail to realize that our growth and potential are dependent on the knowledge that we learn in life. Whatever we produce in life most certainly will affect the children who will carry on our legacy, whatever we choose for it to be. Hopefully they will grow to heights that will make us proud. Yes, idle minds produce negative thoughts that some will live by forever. We are the captains of our ship and we travel on roads that will bear us fruit. Never forget that what we're going through is never as big as we perceive it to be. In all that we do, include the mind. It's a dear friend that we sometimes ignore. Stay focused and you'll reap the fruits of the gift of simply having a mind!

What a Waste!

A mind wasted floats endlessly in the darkness of reality! This powerful organ, the brain, and our thoughts that guide us to prosperity in life will be stilled unless we work it and understand how it works and controls our everyday life. One the surface, we can only see and know what is shallow and the deep messages go unnoticed. But when we learn to go deep into the mind to see and discover all of its possibilities, then and only then will we move up the ladder of life's success and find our purpose. The deeper we go into our own mind, everything is extracted that gives us more of life's secrets. Most leaders of the world have learned the formula to controlling the inner thoughts of mankind. With this method, they get access to the wealth of the world. What's left is what we get. Come on and join me in exploring this new frontier that will bring peace and understanding to a pleasant life!

The Brain

When the brain relaxes too much something happens. It's like an automobile engine that needs oil all of the time. The brain needs stimulation in order to function at its highest level. When the brain shuts down because of despair, depression, fear, death, the loss of a love affair, or anything of value to us, we tend to lose control and the brain, working under the principles that I spoke of earlier, shuts down to a lower state and only deals with the depression and the loss of control that we feel at that time. When we allow ourselves to go the unpredictable route, we in some cases lose touch with reality and some will never return. That's why because we are a creative being we must take control of our destiny. A good brain that functions can withstand any adversity, come what may. We must steer it like a ship on high seas and rough waters just like a captain who is in charge. It has been said that the captain is the last to leave the vessel. We, like the captain, must do everything to make sure our ship doesn't go down!

Our Words

When we speak, our words influence the atmosphere and cannot be taken back. Sometimes we are excused because of what we say and we move on, although the bite is still there! We must think before we speak at all times because the resulting hurt changes the way people feel about us. Words contain a power that can start wars and end them! Words create weddings, correct children, show loved ones that all is well, and also explain the human language. They are used to pray and sing praises! Words are just that powerful! So, when you speak, choose your words carefully because you don't know how they will affect the person that you are speaking to!

P. S. Keep speaking words for most are pleasant to hear! When those same words are put to music what a beautiful sound!!

Defining Choices

We make choices in life that define who we are! Sometimes we change courses in life if we feel that the direction we are traveling is not treating us well. So, we move on, trying to find and make the right connections. Finally, we discover it! The mind and reality find a medium and everything becomes clear. Manhood arrives, goals are set, finances improve, and never again will we see the dark side of life because once life reveals itself, the mind falls in line with it and never let's go!

Thoughts

What are your thoughts today? Of buying a new car, opening a new business, getting married… Well, we all have them but do we really act upon them? Our thoughts, I believe, guide us to life's gifts, dreams, realities, and rewards!

Life's Formula

Don't be confused about life, just focus! Just like an archer aiming his arrow at his target, you can clearly see the real picture of life's formula. There's no secret to receiving your gifts in life, you just have to follow the formula. Remember 2 times 2 equals 4? That's a formula! When you have a thought, does it stay with you for long or does it pass, just to be replaced with a new one? When you learn to hold onto a thought and extract all that you can from it, eventually you will manifest it and all of its knowledge will be retained by you! Now, when you see the same situation again, you will deal with it in a better way. Try this method over and over until you master your thoughts and you will always be excited when another situation comes your way! Just like Sherlock Holmes, with a little detective work, focusing will be your second nature!

Dreaming Again?

Dreams are realistic views of life in a subtle state! When we dream about something of value, it tells us that we are ready to do something amazing for ourselves very soon. How soon? Well, that depends on how well you understand your dream. See yourself in your dreams! See the reality of where you want to be and move on it! Continue to dream and see your dreams as clear as they can be. Before you know it, a new lifestyle emerges and it's up to you to never let it go!

Role Models

Role models are everywhere! Find one! Something learned is better than something talked about! When I surround myself with people of like minds, my awareness moves me to a level of learning. It causes me to speak up and speak out on the events concerning the times in my life that matter the most to me. On the other hand, when I allow myself to be in a circle of men and women who choose not to connect to reality, I see only a measure of myself being displayed! What I am saying is that when our efforts to move forward are sidetracked, it makes it harder to return to a place that serves us well. We must work hard to maintain our goals and our reasons for being what we want to be. We sometimes float through life because of a lack of role models. Actually, I never have one outside of my mother and father. My information from them was always positive! I say, we should allow the gift of life to take on all of the possibilities that lead us to greatness and never forget to pass it on to someone who never understood the value of a role model!

Motivated

Being motivated is the key to success, for we need this energy to boost the brain into doing what we want it to do. When something is energized, a signal is sent to the brain to focus on the subject matter and create what is being focused on. Getting out of bed is a job for some, but if we knew that there was a check in the mailbox, right away, we become motivated! What I'm saying is that we all have the ability to jump start ourselves. Many become laid back because there's no happiness or excitement to pursue. Many people around the world are living in the same way, just moving about their lives, when all around them there's something exciting to see and do. This energy is ours to keep and to use whenever we see fit. We can't lose this gift, for when the brain has nothing to look forward to, it takes a long nap! Don't let it nap for too long, for all of the good things in life will be there when you awake, but everyone else will be that much further ahead of you! This life that we have is precious and we may live a long time, go many places, and see many things. So, we must stay focused and energized to enjoy all of the values of a good life. So, stay focused, living your life to its fullest! As you grow old, you will often smile to yourself and say, "The world doesn't owe me anything!"

Relationships

Don't let an angry heart make you bitter! Your life is worth so much more than that. Lost lovers will always see their loss through the small end of the funnel. When you walk away from a bad experience always stay focused on a new beginning! Never trot again on a similar path for a new road will always take you to a new town. Never let loneliness be your friend. This is a natural reaction. When we are out of a relationship, everything looks dull and nothing seems right. This is only because of what we allow our minds to see and our hearts to feel. The plan for lovers in life is so simple. When in love, stay in love. Do whatever it takes to make this happen. It's a dual commitment and it only works when two horses pull the same cart in the same direction! Right! So, if your relationship goes into a tailspin, go to the Source and ask if the cart is still moving in the right direction. If it's not, ask why, especially if you are unaware of this new turn. Don't feel lost if the answer is not to your liking. When a heavy wind blows everything in its path will move. Keep your ears up, nose open, and your sights on a better day because the foreseeable is what we want, yet the unforeseeable is sometimes what we get!

Memories

Life is full of memories that come and go! Some are good and some are not so good. We keep the ones that make us feel good about a person, a place, or a thing. There are many songs about memories that tell a story of love lost and love won. If it wasn't for memories, we would not have thoughts of yesterday. Memories are keys to daily our functions. We recall colors and we count money all based on memory! When our memory serves us, we travel and return from places that gave us joy. Memories… What a special gift! Some of us still remember how to pray and give thanks for the memories that we hold dear to our hearts!

The Storms of Life

When mental storms come our way, they catch us by surprise! So, what do you do? Will you let them override your good thinking or will you try to properly process them? Storms remind us of the times when we need to prepare for the worst. Some will allow their emotions to guide them or allow fear to overpower their thinking resources. Others will see the storm and latch down until it's over, promising to be prepared for the next time. It's all about being prepared for whatever comes our way. The human body and mind are powerful forces when used to their fullest potential! Our thought processes are ready when called upon and we must know how to use these God-given gifts to prepare, motivate, and think through any situation that we encounter. Yes, the brain will pull you through, but you must cultivate it every day, which is a form of mental exercise. We are the Castle Keeper and we are either going to learn how to maneuver in life, or we'll consistently fail to understand the true power of the Almighty gift of our thoughts to steer us in the right direction!

Respect

We all want it, 24/7! When we ignore this point, we then set ourselves up to be disrespected by others. Everyone has a right to be respected. It takes the harshness out of the air. When we learn this method, it opens the door to the possibilities of a relationship. Look into the mirror when you smile and you will see someone smiling back at you! Likewise, when you frown, someone in the mirror will frown back at you. You see, the image that we project is the image that we will receive. Guess what, life is your mirror! Respect others and over time, they will respect you!

So Much More

Why do we cry when life offers so much more than tears? Choices are ours and ours alone. We can't predict others' behavior. We would like for them to give us the same respect. We all know that this is sometimes wishful thinking. Happy are they that know and follow the rules of love. Be happy! Stay happy! Stay in love! Climb your highest mountain! Swim your deepest sea! Follow your wildest dreams and come full circle with your realities! Then and only then will you reach that plateau where equals fly and the sweet air refreshes your mind to go a little further!

The Wind

Plastic bags are like people, they go wherever the wind blows. You see these bags everywhere, caught in trees, waterways, even blowing in the wind! They get caught in the exhaust pipes of cars. People are the same way! They become entangled in the reels of life and get lost in habits that seem impossible to break! The winds of life blow and everything in its path will dance to the tune of the winds of time!

Reflections

Just thinking back and reviewing life's choices... Can we change what we feel as though will make life a better place? Will our choices make life worst? Reflections and choices make it all come together. Young people make their own choices, for when they leave the house and take on the attitude of the streets, surely their choices will cause realities to form and life will begin to go downhill. Choices are ours to live by. When families are short on teachings and God is nowhere to be found, the structure of the household is dismal and unclear. We must stay in charge of our flock and as shepherds learn to capture the flock that will be tomorrow's future! Respect, reflections, and choices are the keys that will thrust us to the place of fruitful happiness!

Heroes

Life, the precious gift from God, only comes once and we must hold onto every moment with care! Would you give up your life for someone you don't even know? Would you sacrifice it so that another could live? These questions have to mean something to most people because some people will and do give their lives so that others can have a better place in life. These are the ultimate heroes that I speak of today! Many pay little attention to what they may lose, be it family, friends, a wife, children, or a life that they too can enjoy for themselves. Would you be that hero and give of yourself so that others can live? Ask yourself that question and see if the answer will reveal the hero in you! I salute these brave men and women, real heroes of humanity, who leave their homelands to fight for our freedom, unselfishly! These are the true heroes of our time and I will always honor them as such!

Roadmap to Success

Your goals are the road maps that guide you and show you what's possible for your life! Life takes on new meaning when you become motivated to live it! Set some goals and go after them in an unstoppable way! They assist you with channeling your energy to produce a desired action. They actually place you in charge of your life!

A Still Pond

When the mind is idle, it's like a still pond, gathering moss with no ripples! Why? There's no activity to stimulate interest. We need challenges to constantly move the waters and agitate the brain to function! When we become in tune with the inner man, knowledge explodes and a higher learning is released. Think about the people of the world who advance and prosper. All of their gifts come from mental energy flowing from their brain. This energy can only be expressed when we are energized internally! Yet, still, we like the still pond, move only when a slight wind blows. We must be like raging waters, rivers flowing rapidly to the sea, creating waves and ripples! Likewise, we should rush to the shore, hold nothing back, and express full control of our Divine nature! We are to flow endlessly without interruption! Yes, we are mighty rivers proudly doing what we do best, controlling our flow and refusing to be stilled like the pond which collects moss and algae, allowing the sun to dry it out again and again! To you I say, "Think of rivers, ripples, and strong endless flows to the sea of life and its rewards!

Have a Seat!

When we sit down and have a talk with ourselves, we learn many things that are helpful to our well-being such as our health, our loved ones, and more importantly, ourselves. When we listen to the control box, which is the brain, we find that we are not alone in this world because our Creator saw fit to equip us with all that we need to survive in His kingdom on earth. We tend to stray away from this truth and we stumble and fall because the course taken was off of our true path. When we are misaligned, there's no real plan to steer us back and no signs to follow. This takes us deeper into the unknowns of life, not having a road map to help us to return. It's only when we stop and gather our thoughts that we are able to discover the directions that will lead us to where we desire to go. Look around and see the roads that we should travel! Leave the unpaved roads to those who desire to wander through life, searching for more unpaved roads!

Hard Times

When times are hard, we bow to the winds of life and push on! As we push on, we learn that hard times don't last forever. We think through the fog and find answers that can advance us. We must think things through because our wants in life are dependent upon how we think. So, when we reach for the sky, we later reach for the stars, and eventually the universe! We'll soon receive the best that life has to offer! Reach! Reach! Higher! Higher!

Where We Are

Some say moving on is too hard! I say, maybe not. It's our perception that causes us to be where are in life. Comfort zones are just that, a place where we feel that there's no need to go any further. When there's a disconnect, as in relationships, we become withdrawn and make ourselves believe that the loss is too great to bear. We're only looking at the surface of the mind. The protector of all men lies deep inside of a place where reasoning and thought controls all behavior. Some learn quickly the powers of the mind and life moves faster for them. They grow to higher levels financially and personally. If we challenge ourselves every day, the rewards will push us deeper into the realities of mental thinking and when you arrive, life will reveal its true self! You too will discover that the education of self is worth the trip after all!

Life

My son, life has blasted us all with unpleasant horrors, yet we still move on. We want things in life to be as we think of them. This is only a fantasy because of the differences that we all have. We must see through the eyes of our own possibilities and the gifts that we want for ourselves. This life can be a good one, a life that we can share with our families and special friends, not trying to change the world or cause people to see what we see. When people shun what you are saying, it doesn't mean that what we are saying is wrong. It means that they don't see the vision that you hold. When we see this disconnect, we must smile to ourselves and say, "I see what you don't see and because of it, I excel to a level that makes my life that much more pleasing to me! I seek people with like minds and ideas and I grow to levels beyond belief! This is the true formula!

Quiet Places

Driving down the highway of my life, I see many things! Some I can change and some I can't. The ones that I can I will, which are the ones that are most related to me. My inner drives and motivations are keys that I need to unlock many doors that are before me. In order to see my passions, I must learn from my mind's experiences and pay attention to the subtle waves that produce my thoughts. It's important to me to find quiet places to sit down and reflect on the events of the day and to prepare for the events of tomorrow. These quiet times are waiting for us all to learn our real purpose in the world full of God's creations. When we discover our true self worth, we will begin to live within these new discoveries. Our true identity will become our reality, never to be washed away again by others! Now we have secured the spirit of the man who has found a place to dwell in alongside his human temple. This will then control the inner man who is looking through the eyes, the pilots, that navigate the paths to bring us happiness, prosperity, and peace that's next to none!

Real Purpose

Many think that their life here on earth has no real purpose! They move about taking all of life's blows. I say, not so! When we travel through life without connecting with the Spirit or our mental ability, then we become a wanderer, seeking pleasure without effort. Challenge, faith, and commitment to self are the keys to life's abundance. Ask this question of most people who have reached success in life, "How did you get to where you are in life today? The answer will always be consistent work, setting goals, and staying true to them. When these guidelines are broken, you will surely have to start over. Everything in life has a formula, whether it's mixing chemicals or preparing food. All of the ingredients must mix together. Look around and see the message that I speak of here. Wanderers… creating monsters and demons all throughout their lives until the laws that govern us all shut down. I say, leave a gift in this world for others to believe in and as life moves on, it will be a little bit better for someone else!

Be Remembered

Ever hear the saying that people will soon forget you? This may be true, but they never forget how you make them feel. We never know what memories we will leave behind in the minds of others. People will remember the good ones first! You don't have to be rich to be thought of. Your deeds alone will secure that memory. Our senses control everything and our unselfish behaviors are the roadways to the hearts of others!

Investment

Ever invest in yourself lately? Tell yourself that you're worth every bit of time that you put into yourself. Did you stop feeling that way or will you continue to grow for the purpose of self? Remember, we all carry our own ball and we shovel our own snow. So now, how do you feel about moving on? Open your eyes and let your brain see the path that it must follow. Two things that will grant you your prize, eyes open and brains functioning!

Limitless

Are we testing our limits? Do we know that we can go further than where we are right now? Most people live within their limitations. We learn early on in life to work late, earn money, buy a house, a car, and get married. Is that all there is to life? We understand from the Bible that God is infallible and his mercy is infinite. We were made by a perfect God who has no limits and I believe that this is passed on to the children of that same God. I know there's more and I must prove it to myself that what I am seeking is also seeking me! I will find my place in this world because I have a lifetime to do it!

Free to Choose

It's funny how we change our feelings from happy to sad and don't know how to reverse these feelings that could eventually destroy us. Sadness is a state of mind that can be reversed, but we become mentally ill when life takes a turn! It's human nature to want life's situations to favor us all of the time. When the spinning bottles of reality point to us, we are not prepared to deal with the challenge. Controlling the mind will clarify the thoughts and feelings and help to sort through life's rocky roads. We are the head of all that we think and do in this life. We must remember that every day brings new highs and new lows. Our thinking process is a daily undertaking. We must be prepared to use our God-given tool, the mind!

The Left Behinds

The world is changing! New ways of thinking are everywhere. People are learning more and they are prospering more. What about the left behinds? Will they prosper too or will this new wave be just business as usual? It's been proven that every man must shovel his own snow. We can read a lot into that statement for sure. We all know how we got into this situation in the first place, but we don't have to stay here. I really don't think so! What's missing? The BIG picture is having the ability to see beyond what you're looking at! This is the future mind at work. We've got to shake this dreamy state of mind and know that there's life ahead of us. We must challenge everyone if we're going to be in the lineup, ahead of the left behind's!

I'll Fly Away!

One day I'll fly away and leave this place that I call home, a place where love has gone to places unknown. Yes, home is where the heart is but now it's gone. As I move through life, I see many things that are cold and careless. People are wandering through the streets with no real purpose and some with no hope. Yes, life can be better than this and someday we must prove it to ourselves that dreams are not impossible. Following my thoughts into a better life carries me deeper into the world of possibilities. Seeing visions of hope and challenges are clearly the focus of a man that wants so much more. Sometimes we need to fly away over the tree tops, down into the valley, and over the mountains. Move on, take your flight and keep your heart, mind, and vision open to the world where dreams become realities and hearts are warmed again! Yes, fly my friends, and never look back to see the darkness that pushed you into flight in the first place. Oh, look at the green fields and smell the wild flowers in the meadows!

ACKNOWLEDGEMENTS

I want to thank my daughter, Toni Hatton, for letting me take her on this journey of the mind! Many times we talked on the phone, late into the night. I would ask her, "How does this story sound, Toni?" She would say, "Dad, I really like that one!" She would type every word as I spoke it to her over the phone, thousands of words! Here we are at 3 books, stories that tell of love, hate, life, death, family, friends, young children lost to a world that they know little of, and the powers of the mind to accomplish the impossible! I hope these messages pertaining to life's lessons will reach the young people of today, in my lifetime, and that the village will once again see the love of the elders that I remember while growing up in my town!

Master Your Mind!

1. What are your first thoughts in the morning?

_____

_____

_____

_____

_____

_____

_____

_____

2. When you experience the unexpected, what are the first words that you say?

_____

_____

_____

_____

_____

_____

3. How do you feel most of the time?

_____

_____

_____

_____

_____

_____

4. What should you be thinking about in order to produce what you desire in life?

_____

_____

_____

_____

_____

_____

_____

5. List 5 things that you can do right now to get you closer to your goals!

_____

_____

_____

_____

_____

_____

www.ingramcontent.com/pod-product-compliance
Lightning Source LLC
Chambersburg PA
CBHW020951090426
42736CB00010B/1359